KEYS TO PARENTING KIDS WITH AUTISM:

The Journey of a Heroic Parent

Shelley Harrison

Table of contents

Chapter 1:

Introduction

I applaud your efforts to support and comprehend your special needs child as they navigate life. As a parent of an autistic child, you likely experience the tumult of emotions, demands, and worries that go along with this difficulty. You're not alone. Statistics show that 1 in 100 children in the US has autism spectrum disorder (ASD), according to a study conducted by the US Center for Disease Control and Prevention in 2009. This statistic suggests that many parents care for their kid who has ASD. As a parent of a child who has just received a diagnosis, you can be confident that having solid knowledge and skills will give you the advantage of being able to put the puzzle pieces together to help your child lead a fulfilling and happy life. After all, it has been proven that children with ASD or any other type of special need can lead meaningful, productive, and rewarding lives.

This book has been thoughtfully written to help you learn a great deal about kids with ASD and how to connect with and understand your kid. The sentiments and emotions of the parents or caregivers are also addressed in this book. Here, you will discover how to strike a balance between providing care for your child and looking after yourself to remain strong and resilient.

Chapter 2:

The Truth About Autism Spectrum Disorder: Symptoms Explained

Before we continue, I would like you to pay special attention to the following important details listed below:

- Autism, often known as autism spectrum disorder, refers to a wide range of diseases that affect how the brain develops.
- Autism affects around 1 in 100 children.
- Early infancy may allow for the detection of some traits, however, autism is frequently not diagnosed until much later.
- People with autism have a variety of skills and requirements, which might change over time.
- Although some autistic individuals may live independently, others have significant difficulties and need ongoing care and assistance.

- Evidence-based psychosocial therapies have a favorable effect on the well-being and quality of life of autistic persons as well as their carers through enhancing communication and social skills.

What is Autism spectrum disorder?

A range of neurodevelopmental disorder. A developmental disability that has an impact on how people behave, learn, and interact with others in social situations. People may exhibit recurring, distinctive behavioral patterns or specific interests. These symptoms, which are often present from early childhood and have an impact on everyday functioning, may not be present in all individuals with ASD. ASD may affect both children and adults.

The word "spectrum" describes the vast variety of symptoms, abilities, and degrees of functional dysfunction that can exist in individuals with ASD. While some children and people with ASD are entirely capable of carrying out all everyday activities, others need significant assistance to do even the most basic tasks. Extreme intellectual prowess and severe assistance are both possible in learning and thinking. Asperger syndrome, childhood disintegrative disorder, and pervasive developmental disorders not otherwise specified (PDD-NOS) are all classified as parts of autism spectrum disorder (ASD) in the Diagnostic and Statistical Manual of Mental Disorders. An evaluation of intellectual disability and linguistic impairment is part of an ASD diagnosis.

Every racial and ethnic group, as well as people from various socioeconomic backgrounds, experience ASD. However, compared to females, boys have a much higher risk of developing ASD.

What are a few typical ASD symptoms?

Children with ASD may appear different even as babies, especially when compared to other kids their same age. They could fixate on a few things excessively, seldom establish eye contact, and refrain from chattering to their parents as they normally would. In other instances, kids could grow normally up until their second or third birthday, but after that, they might start to retreat and lose interest in social interaction.

The degree to which a person's everyday functioning is impacted by repetitive patterns of behavior, insistence on sameness in activities and settings, and social communication issues can determine how severe an ASD diagnosis is. The warning indicators are as follows:

Social dysfunction and communication issues
The difficulty of social relationships is common among those with ASD. Common communication and interaction's give-and-take dynamic can be particularly difficult. Children with ASD may not acknowledge their names, avoid making eye contact with others, and only interact with others to further their own interests. Children with ASD may prefer to be alone since they frequently don't know how to play or interact with other kids. It may be challenging for someone with ASD to relate to others' emotions or discuss their own.

People with ASD may speak in a variety of ways, from barely speaking at all to speaking fluently but in socially unacceptable ways. Some ASD kids may repeat words and phrases, provide illogical responses to inquiries, and have delayed speech and language development. Additionally, individuals with ASD may struggle to use and comprehend non-verbal signs such gestures, body language, and tone of voice. Young toddlers with ASD, for instance, could not comprehend what it means to wave goodbye. People with ASD may also have a flat, robotic, or sing-song voice and speak about a small number of their preferred subjects without much respect for the listener's interests.

Recurrent and distinctive behaviors
Many kids with ASD exhibit strange or repetitive activities, such as flapping their arms, swaying from side to side, or spinning. They could start to focus on certain details of things, like the wheels on a toy truck. Children may develop an obsessional interest in a particular subject, such as trains or aircraft, for example. Changes to everyday routines, such as an unexpected halt on the way home from school, may be quite difficult for many persons with ASD who seem to thrive on predictability. Some kids could even lose

their temper or experience emotional outbursts, especially if they are in an unfamiliar or too stimulating setting.

What conditions are connected to ASD?

Fragile X syndrome, which results in intellectual disability, and tuberous sclerosis, which causes benign tumors to grow in the brain and other vital organs, are two known genetic disorders that are linked to an increased risk for autism. Each of these disorders is caused by a mutation in a single, distinct gene. In recent years, scientists have found other genetic alterations in autistic youngsters, some of which have not yet been termed diseases. Even though each of these illnesses is uncommon, together they may be responsible for 20% or more of all instances of autism.

The likelihood of developing seizures is also higher than usual in those with ASD. Before the age of three, children who have language regression appear to be at increased risk of epilepsy or brain activity that resembles seizures. By the time they are adults, 20 to 30 percent of children with ASD have seizures. Additionally, seizure disorders are most likely to occur in persons with ASD and intellectual impairment.

How is ASD identified?

Depending on how severe the illness is, ASD symptoms can differ substantially from person to person. For young children with moderate ASD or other less severe disabilities, symptoms may potentially go unnoticed.

The Diagnostic and Statistical Manual of Mental Illnesses-V, a manual developed by the American Psychiatric Association for the diagnosis of mental disorders, states that autism spectrum disorder is diagnosed by clinicians based on symptoms, signs, and tests. Children should undergo routine screenings for developmental delays, and in particular, for autism, at their 18- and 24-month well-child visits.

Very early warning signs that necessitate professional assessment include:
By age 1, there is no babbling or pointing.
At 16 months, no single words, and by 2 years, no two-word sentences.
No reaction to the name
Loss of previously learned language or social abilities
Missing eye contact
Excessive toy or item lining up
No grin or attempt at social interaction

Other warning signs include:
Difficulty forming friendships with classmates.
Impairment in one's capacity to start or carry on a discussion with others
Lack of or diminished capacity for imaginative and social play

Preoccupation with certain items or themes
Repetitive or unconventional language usage Abnormally strong or focused attention
Rigid adherence to predetermined procedures or rituals

A more thorough assessment is typically recommended if screening tools suggest the potential of ASD. A multidisciplinary team composed of a psychologist, neurologist, psychiatrist, speech therapist, and other specialists who diagnose and treat ASD in children is necessary for a thorough examination. A comprehensive neurological evaluation as well as in-depth cognitive and linguistic tests will be performed by the team members. Children with delayed speech development should also have their hearing evaluated since hearing issues might result in behaviors that could be misconstrued for ASD.

Why Does ASD Occur?

ASD is thought to be influenced by both genetics and environment, according to scientists. The fact that autism rates have been rising in recent decades without a clear explanation for why is causing tremendous concern. Numerous genes linked to the illness have been discovered by researchers. Those with ASD exhibit different patterns of brain growth, according to imaging studies. According to studies, changes in normal brain growth very early in development may be the cause of ASD. These disruptions might be the result of genetic flaws that affect the genes that direct brain development and control intercellular communication. Children who were born too soon are more likely to have autism. Despite the fact that no particular environmental causes have yet been found, environmental variables may potentially affect how genes operate and evolve. It has long been proven that parenting styles do not cause autism spectrum disorder (ASD).

Numerous studies have demonstrated that immunization against infectious illnesses in children does not raise the population's risk of autism.

What function do genes serve?
Twin and family studies are compelling evidence that certain people are predisposed to autism genetically. According to studies of identical twins, the likelihood that the other twin would experience the same problem as the first twin ranges from 36 to 95 percent. Numerous research are being conducted to identify the precise genetic variables connected to the emergence of ASD. The likelihood of having a second kid with ASD increases in homes where there is already one affected child. Numerous genes discovered to be linked to autism play a role in how the chemical connections between brain neurons function (synapses). Finding hints about the genes that promote vulnerability is a goal of research. Sometimes the parents or other family

members of an ASD kid exhibit modest communication disorders in social situations or engage in repetitive actions. Evidence also points to a higher than usual prevalence of emotional illnesses in the relatives of persons with ASD, including bipolar disorder and schizophrenia.

De novo, or spontaneous, gene mutations have also been demonstrated to affect the likelihood of developing autism spectrum disorder, in addition to inherited genetic abnormalities that are found in virtually all of a person's cells. De novo mutations, which can happen spontaneously in a parent's sperm or egg cell or after conception, are alterations in DNA sequences, the human body's genetic material. Then, when the fertilized egg divides, the mutation takes place in each cell. These mutations might damage a single gene or they can cause what are known as copy number variations, which include the deletion or duplication of sections of DNA that contain many genes. Recent research has shown that individuals with ASD tend to have more copy number de novo gene mutations than individuals without the disorder, which suggests that for some individuals, the risk of developing ASD may not be caused by mutations in specific genes but rather by spontaneous coding mutations across a number of genes. De novo mutations may be used to explain genetic illnesses in which the afflicted kid carries the mutation in every cell but none of the parents do, and in which the disorder does not run in the family. Children born to parents who are older are likewise more likely to have autism. To ascertain the possible impact of environmental variables on spontaneous mutations and how it affects the risk of ASD, there is still more study to be done.

Do autistic symptoms evolve over time?
Many children's symptoms go better as they become older and get behavioral therapy.

Some adolescents with ASD may develop depression or behavioral issues at this time, and their therapy may need to be modified as they get older. However, depending on the severity of the disorder, people with ASD may be able to work successfully, live independently, or live in a supportive environment. People with ASD typically continue to need services and supports as they age.

How does autism therapy work?
There is currently no treatment for ASD. Specific symptoms can be significantly improved with the use of therapies and behavioral interventions, which are intended to treat particular symptoms. Medication can be used to address certain symptoms. The best treatment strategy coordinates treatments and therapies to address each patient's unique requirements. The majority of medical experts concur that the earlier the intervention, the better.

I hope the information I provided was useful. Though we may be familiar with these things, we must refresh our memory to fully comprehend this book. See you in the next chapter.

Chapter 3:

Quick Note: General Misconceptions about ASD

- Autism is a disease
- Autism may result from poor parenting.
- People with autism do not experience emotion
- People with autism cannot learn.
- Autism can improve with time.
- Vaccinations lead to autism
- Autism is spreading like wildfire.
- Autistic persons are more violent since they cannot talk

The sooner you ignore everything above, the better for you. I've observed parents continually place the responsibility for their child's situation on themselves. I wish to correct that highly incorrect assumption since it is one. No parent is to blame for their child's autism. So instead of blaming yourself, you come up with fresh methods to love and support your child.

Chapter 4:

Recognizing The Child Behind The Symptoms

Every autistic person has distinctive behaviors and traits, according to a common phrase. This means that a kid with autism may behave differently from other autistic children. This is why it's critical to identify your child's unique characteristics from a young age.

Since autism carries a lot of stigmas and is sometimes described as a "life-ruiner" for parents who don't understand it, receiving an autism diagnosis for your kid may leave you feeling stunned, bewildered, terrified, and unclear of how to proceed. But autism is not a "life-ruiner"; rather, it is more of a game-changer.

The process of learning for your kid with special needs can be emotionally taxing. The path is often fraught with difficulties and demands, such as continuing therapy, programs, plans for special schooling, and medical care. I want to remove even another layer and talk about a subject that is often ignored yet needs consideration and compassion. I want to talk about how it feels to have a special needs kid that doesn't appear to appreciate your love, care, and attention.

Although you are aware that your child's impairment makes it difficult for them to show their love, on a maternal or paternal level, it might seem terrible. It may seem like watering a planter to feed a bud of a flower if your kid engages in difficult, defiant, or destructive behaviors, to take this a step further. On some days, you can see and feel the blossom developing, but on other days, no matter how much water you add, it appears to just drain out the bottom of the pot.

Always keep in mind that your youngster is trying their best. They would improve if they could. Due to their disability, your kid may face additional challenges, which they may find taxing and frustrating. Like you, they are giving it their all.

Even when it seems like your kid is acting inappropriately, there are valid reasons for it. Your kid is not attempting to "act out" or get into trouble. Your kid will see the world differently than you do, and as a result, their responses to it will be unique from yours.

Let your kid be special. They are not required to move, play, talk, eat, or engage in the same manner as youngsters who are not autistic. You and your kid will experience stress if you demand that they do it. Remove the pressure and allow them to be unique.

It may be painful when others behave as if it's awful that your kid is different. Recall that they are in error.

Think about the kid you now have. Dispel "what-ifs" about the kid you may have had who wasn't autistic and stop worrying so much about what your child might turn out to be. You currently have a youngster with you. They want to know that you are proud of them and that you love them as much as they love you.

Attempt to achieve attainable objectives like teaching Anna to say yes and no or getting her to utilize AAC. Think about your child's current situation and what they can do next. Consider Anna's employment potential while setting objectives, if your kid is old enough.
Work through issues with your kid. You may talk with your kid about what is happening if they can speak or use AAC. Talk to them and find out what they believe the issue is and how you two might be able to resolve it. Sometimes they could provide insightful information.

Give some leeway for weirdness. Your child doesn't need to spend their formative years attempting to fit in with the crowd. It's

acceptable if they have peculiar movements, rely on AAC rather than speech, or enjoy chewing on toys. You and your child will become frustrated and worn out if you attempt to control every movement.
In general, if a peculiarity doesn't harm anyone, leave it alone.
You can work on it if it is harming others or yourself (by disrupting a lesson or destroying things, for example).

Support your child's sense of self-worth. Your child can hear what people are saying, despite the appearance to the contrary (unless they are deaf). Be careful what you say when people are nearby. Don't forget to talk about both their strengths and faults, congratulate their successes (even if they don't occur by the developmental schedule), and express your pride in them.
Be there for them if they fall into the self-hatred trap and think about getting therapy.

Allow your kid to play. Don't give in to the urge to have your kid work hard for long hours every day; childhood should include time for play. Your kid needs lots of downtimes, and it's unpleasant to share your home with a youngster who has had a week of exhausting therapy sessions. Allow children to engage in independent play every day, even if it seems strange to you.
Children with autism need a lot of downtimes to prevent harmful stress buildups.

Spend time together as a family. Set aside some time for exploration, hanging out, or conversation, but not for therapy. Every encounter doesn't need to have a purpose. Take a laugh together.
Find out whether your kid enjoys a particular fitness activity, such as walking, swimming, or playing catch. These may be completed together.

Honor your child's talents and qualities. A single-minded emphasis on flaws is boring. Praise your child's accomplishments and motivate them to concentrate on their strengths and favorite activities.
Starting with your child's unique interests is a smart idea. Encourage them to research their chosen topics and practice the necessary skills (reading, bug catching, playing music, et cetera).

I'll give you room to think about these guidelines and how you can adhere them.

Chapter 5:

Understanding Your Child's Emotions

It's a misconception that autistic youngsters exhibit little to no emotion. Nothing is more false than it is. Children with autism may experience emotions for various causes or express them in various ways, but they nonetheless experience the same range of emotions as everyone else.

Children with autism may occasionally display even greater emotional sensitivity than some of their usual peers. However, they may struggle to communicate their emotions and might need assistance.

The way that autistic children think, speak, and act differs from that of their regular peers. They frequently exhibit extreme self-absorption and seem more concerned with flicking their fingers or lining up objects than they do with playing or engaging with others. When a child doesn't start play, ask questions, participate in sports, or desire to try new things, how are parents supposed to interact with them? Here are some suggestions for parents who wish to build a close bond with their autistic child but don't know where to begin.

Don't Assume What Your Child Is Thinking or Feeling

Most of the time, by observing someone's face, hearing their speech, or observing their body language, you can infer what they are experiencing. However, those with autism may not talk at all or may speak in a flat tone even when they are excited. Even more difficult to master is body language, which includes eye contact, appropriate movements, and facial expressions. Never assume that your youngster isn't having fun because of a flat tone, lack of eye contact, or difficulty focusing. Your presumptions are likely incorrect.

Exercise Initiative

Many young youngsters can't wait to play with their parents. A lot of parents find it extremely tiresome to hear requests like "Mommy, come play" or "Daddy, you be the monster and pursue me."

Most parents of autistic children would give anything to hear that kind of request. This isn't because kids with autism don't like chase games or spending time with Mommy; rather, it's because they lack the abilities to visualize what they want, express that vision verbally, and convey their goals. Therefore, it is up to you, the parent, to start the game. Let your youngster hear from you instead of waiting to hear from them. Let your body speak by demonstrating the type of play you have in mind if they have trouble understanding spoken instructions like "Let's play with catch."

Expand Your Child's Interests

The imposition of a parent's interests on their child is common, and it can even be done quite successfully. Mom enjoys dressing up, so she buys her daughter dress-up outfits so that she can share in

Mom's pleasure. Dad joins Little League because he loves baseball, and the experience is amazing.

Since autistic children's interests are less adaptable than those of regular kids, it can be difficult to encourage them to participate in your favorite activities. Focusing on your child's preferences instead of your own is a wiser move. Is your kid a fan of model trains? Discover your inner railfan. Is Sesame Street his obsession? Learn the reason Big Bird is so popular! You'll discover new opportunities to play and connect as you figure out how to interact vocally or nonverbally with your youngster about his hobbies.

Think Creatively and Outside the Box

Autism makes it unlikely that many kids will be interested in common pursuits like team sports. Your autistic youngster does not, however, lack hobbies. Take note of what your youngster says and does, and think about engaging in unconventional activities.

A few options include dancing and acting, going for walks in the woods, going to concerts, and even fishing.

Engage your father, brothers, or uncles
Children with autism much too frequently end up in a world dominated by women. This occurs for many good reasons, including the fact that mothers are more likely to seek careers as early childhood teachers and therapists and are typically more active in their special needs child's daily care and program and therapy selection.
The fact that fathers of autistic sons are frequently turned off by their son's lack of interest in stereotypically masculine activities like team sports, using tools, and so on, however, is a much more important problem. Many men back off because they are unsure of how to relate to their sons, letting Mom take the initiative and missing out on the chance to connect. However, by following your child's lead and considering

alternatives (hiking instead of baseball, for instance), you may discover several shared interests that are just beyond the norm.

Avoid quitting too soon

People with autism typically dislike change a lot. Some autistic individuals outright despise change. As a result, introducing anything new, whether it be a new movie, activity, game, or location, might take a very long period. Although it doesn't imply you have to keep doing the same things forever, it does mean that you, as the parent, need to have a lot of patience. Start by describing the new activity in words and visuals. After that, involve your child in brief, simple steps.

Raising the bar

It is simple to keep doing the same thing with your autistic child over and over again since parents get tired. After all, he likes it and you can do it easily. However, you miss the chance to develop a close bond with your child when you let sameness rule your interactions with her. Yes, it's okay to indulge in preferred pastimes. Who doesn't appreciate reading a favorite book aloud or returning year after year to the same attractions at the same theme park? But it's crucial to keep in mind that, like all kids, your autistic child is developing and changing. It is up to you as the parent to assist your child in reaching the subsequent level of competence and maturity because he may not demand change or even desire it. 25 times in a row, has he created the identical circular train layout? It's time to include a bridge, a tunnel, a barrier, or a new path. A change could take some time to seem natural, but that's alright because you're all learning together.

Be Happy with Your Child's Successes:

Your autistic child could or might not end up being an "achiever" in the traditional meaning of the word. He probably won't receive an academic or athletic award or be the focus of the class play if he has a relatively low functioning level (though you never know: stranger things have happened). But each time your autistic child surpasses his previous boundaries, he does something amazing. It's an occasion to rejoice when your youngster asks a question, shares a toy, experiments on his own, or interacts with a stranger.

You might think you can't play with your autistic child if you haven't constructed with blocks, played chase games, colored, or watched Sesame Street in a while. But if you had those play skills as a kid (and chances are you did!), you can get them back and teach them to your autistic child.

Chapter 6:

Helping Your Child Understand His Emotions

Children with autism may require assistance to recognize, comprehend, and control their emotions.

Labels, emotions cards, and ladder images are techniques for assisting kids in recognizing emotions. Explaining the connection between ideas and feelings can aid autistic people in understanding emotions.

Children with autism may need assistance learning how to control and control their powerful emotions.

For instance, your autistic kid may experience unpleasant or negative feelings such as rage. Or they may not be able to tell when they are enthusiastic. Or they would categorize all difficult-to-describe feelings as "being bored."

Children with autism may also need assistance to recognize, understand, and react correctly to other people's emotions. Your autistic kid, for instance, would not notice when someone else is perplexed, sad, or furious. They might also mistakenly believe that someone upset is mad at them because they see them.

The first step in assisting children in learning about emotions is to work on increasing their awareness of their own and other people's feelings.

Identifying emotions: You may teach autistic children about emotions via regular encounters. The following suggestions are for your autistic child:

As you experience emotions during the day, name them. Whether you're reading, watching TV, or seeing pals, you may describe your feelings. For instance, "Look, Katy's is grinning. She is happy

Identify your child's feelings. For instance, "You're grinning. You have to be joyful.

Put a focus on your emotional reactions. For instance, "I'm SO happy!" Please high-five me.

Assist your youngster in understanding how their body responds to emotions. For instance, "You seem anxious. Do you experience an unsettling sensation in your stomach?

Show the parts of the body where people experience emotion by drawing them, such as sweaty palms or a racing heart.

Request that your youngster illustrate their feelings.

Encourage your youngster to play with their emotions. Messy play, drawing or painting, puppet play, dancing, and music play are some play ideas to build emotions in preschoolers and play ideas to develop emotions in school-age children. Play a game about emotions with your kid. You choose a feeling, such as "enthusiastic," and you both embody it. This exercise may be changed into a straightforward guessing game.

For your autistic kid, you may find the following emotional skills helpful:

You may use emotion cards, which include images of faces that are either real or cartoons, to educate your kid about fundamental emotions.

Children with autism between the ages of 2 and 8 may learn about emotions via the animated series The Transporters.

Children with autism may learn about social situations via social storytelling and comic strip talks. For your youngster, a tale or comic strip about emotions could be helpful.

Identifying emotions Preteens and teens with autism

Even while autistic preteens and adolescents may be familiar with the vocabulary for emotions, they often struggle to recognize them in others and themselves, especially when they're sad. They could also find it challenging to read body language, tone of voice, or facial emotions in others.

As suggestions, consider these:
Identify your child's feelings. Start with simpler emotions like joy, fear, and rage before moving on to more complex ones like resentment, jealousy, or shame. I can tell that you're frustrated, you may remark. Have difficulties with that guitar chord?
Encourage your kid to explain physical feelings. For instance, you may say that it feels like a "blender in their gut" if your youngster is anxious. Or you might mention how their heart beats more quickly when they are afraid.
Make emotional observations on fictional characters. You might watch Inside Out together and discuss how the characters' actions reflect their emotions, for instance.

Recognizing and embracing feelings:
It might be easier for your autistic kid to accept their feelings if they know why they feel the way they do.
By explaining to your kid how ideas may result in emotions, you can help them

comprehend why they feel the way they do. For instance, you and a kid may create a picture of a dog. Then you may explain, "You'll feel afraid if a dog leaps up at you and you fear it's going to bite." However, if you imagine what a happy, lively dog it is, you can experience excitement instead.

To assist your youngster to connect emotions with ideas and behavior, you may also utilize comic strip talks including characters with a range of expressions and thinking bubbles. To represent a dialogue, you may, for instance, create stick figures of your kid and a friend. Use various colors to convey what they are feeling, thinking, and expressing.
Your youngster must learn that everyone feels a variety of emotions as part of developing knowledge of them. You may remark, for instance, "It's natural to experience many kinds of emotions, including happiness, sadness, excitement, and jealousy. Feelings may vary in size from

large to little. All of these emotions are normal. It could be beneficial to discuss how strong emotions will dissipate with time.

Managing emotions: Adolescents and children with autism may find it difficult to cope with intense feelings. They often need assistance to control intense emotions and find peace after them. However, kids might pick up strategies to control these feelings.

Relaxing activities
Try relaxing techniques with your kid to discover what works for them. For instance, they may count to ten, take five deep breaths, or focus on a cheerful or calming thought.

They might also try concentrating on their breathing by using their fingers. Your youngster carefully circles their hand with a finger, breathing in when they reach the tip of a finger and out when they reach the bottom. Repeat for each of the ten fingers.

Stimulatory perception
If your kid is feeling happy or furious, they may clap their hands or clutch a cushion or a sensory item. Stimming or using fidget toys from a sensory kit may also be beneficial.

If your kid exhibits inappropriate sensory-seeking behaviors, you may be able to substitute another behavior that satisfies the same sensory demand. If your youngster rockers, for instance, they may use a rocking chair instead. If they want to choose their skin, they may instead tinker with rings, a bracelet, or transparent nail paint.

Break period
Your youngster could take a stroll, grab a sip of water, or choose a peaceful spot to relax.

Alteration of activity
Help your kid take a mental break by listening to their favorite music, reading a

book, or tuning into a podcast on their hobbies.

Try physical exercise
Your youngster could run for a brief period, kick a ball, do pushups, or shoot some hoops.

When your kid is really unhappy, it might be difficult for them to apply these coping mechanisms. They could yell, smash objects, act violently, or act in a challenging manner. You may need to assist autistic kids and teens in certain circumstances to prevent or control meltdowns.

Getting support for emotional growth
Your youngster may learn to recognize and control their emotions with the aid of an accomplished expert. Discussing therapy and supports for autistic children and teens with your child's general practitioner, pediatrician, psychologist, or other health specialists is an excellent beginning step.

Chapter 7:

Managing Your Emotions
The issue about providing care is that it may wear on anybody; it takes patience and understanding. And one may add that having an autistic kid means you have to have thick skin to survive each day.

Here's what I'm not going to say: I'm not going to advise you to keep your mouth shut or to stop grumbling. Instead, I want you to know that being weary is perfectly normal since you are a person. You have the right to experience these human feelings, thus it's OK to seek a break or to return to the past.

But I want you to know that there is no going back; instead, there are things you can do to help you manage these feelings, lighten your load a bit, and allow you to continue enjoying caring for your kid.

Here are some ideas to keep your mind active:

Ensure your wellbeing. You must maintain peak physical and mental health as a caregiver to be able to handle the obstacles that arise daily. This is taking your time and finding methods to look after yourself so that you have enough of yourself (physically, psychologically, and emotionally) to share with others.

Be less stressed. ASD parents often experience higher levels of stress than parents of children with other disorders. Caretakers may experience relationship breakdowns and even psychiatric problems if the problem is not addressed. Your health might also be impacted by stress. Keep your affairs to keep from being overburdened. This entails setting aside time each day for oneself. Among the crucial and even enjoyable methods to achieve it are:

Determine the true origins of your stress. If you're feeling overwhelmed, divide your main problems into smaller, more manageable portions. You'll have a strategy and feel better.

Other options include meditation. Be mindful of your inner dialogue as much as your ideas. You'll be able to eliminate pointless concerns.

Exercise. You are not required to visit the gym. Swim, exercise in the yard, dance in the kitchen, or just go for a walk. These are quick and efficient methods to work out.

Take an exercise class if you want some adult companionship. It's a fantastic way to make new friends and get your energy back.

Go to sleep. There is no substitute for a restful night's sleep when it comes to rejuvenating your body and mind. Use meditation or relaxation techniques to aid in your relaxation if necessary. That might aid in getting your body ready for sleep.

Be inventive with your cuisine. You probably put a lot of effort into making sure your kid eats well-balanced meals. How are you doing? Consider experimenting with new fruits, vegetables, and cuisines to spice up your unique food. To keep things fresh, look for new recipes. and adhere to a daily eating routine. You can keep your system on track and your energy levels up.

Get your life in order. This is the secret to overcoming obstacles in life while maintaining a good standard of living. You and your family will all gain. Schedule some time each week for mingling and having fun. To bring balance to your hectic days, try these suggestions:

Locate your pals. You do have a kid with special needs. But you are also a person. Being aware of your individuality helps you be a better parent. Spend some time laughing and reuniting with your buddies. You'll be happy that you did.

rekindle previous interests. Find your knitting needles, clean the piano, or take the golf clubs out of the bag. Try out some new hobbies that interest you.

Read blogs written by people who care about autistic kids. Reading about other happy families may be beneficial and serve as a reminder to maintain a good outlook. You may ask for assistance in certain online groups, which can be quite beneficial.

Go on a break. Simply said, being a parent is tough labor. Inquire about babysitters locally or abroad by asking around. The prospect of spending more time with her grandkids may make grandma ecstatic. You might also check into the respite options that are available to parents of children with disabilities. This might allow you to rest and rejuvenate.

Whenever you feel overwhelmed, go away from the internet. It's OK to ignore comments and be quiet for a time online. When you have more energy, you may return.

Respect your sleep. A rested parent will be happier and more productive than a zombie from lack of sleep. Use white noise, avoid using electronics before bed, follow a regular bedtime routine, and don't be afraid to use sleep aids if necessary (for yourself or your child). Reduce light and noise in the home around night if your kid has trouble sleeping, and get them checked for any underlying disorders that could be interfering with their sleep (such as epilepsy). Supplemental melatonin may also be useful.

Join a support group. Lean on your family, friends, and anybody else who can assist you get through difficult times. Parenting need not be a lone endeavor.

Allow yourself to feel tough feelings. It's OK to feel angry, perplexed, anxious, or depressed. Being afraid is common. Spend some quiet time thinking things out on your own or with other adults. Exercise, participate in sports, enjoy music, or do anything else that makes you feel better.

Only express your annoyance when you are positive that your youngster is not present. You don't want to find out that they were there and understood every word, leading them to believe that "Mommy hates me."

If you are going through a very tough moment, think about getting treatment for yourself.

Give up striving to be the ideal parent. It's not healthy for you or your kid's health to put 110 percent of your effort into teaching your youngster every day. Allow for the flaws in your family. Allow yourself to relax. You're doing it incorrectly if you're continually fighting to push your kid to accomplish more. Let up. For once, allow yourself and your youngster to unwind. It will be alright.

Chapter 8:

A word?

Permit me to offer these few words of encouragement

You're not alone,as a parent who drives her child to ABA treatment while her pals drop off their kids at ballet rehearsals.

I salute the mother who is always eager to learn more

Your kid is great exactly the way he is. This goes to the parent who avoids milestone discussions with his friends because his child is years behind.

To the parent who is feeling humiliated as your son's screams at the parking lot, you're not alone

You are your child's best advocate, a parent who is scouring the internet for the right sort of treatment for her kid.

I understand that it's challenging for dads who are reluctant to take their kids to restaurants, parks, or other public places. It may not turn out the way you imagined it, but it will.

To the woman who is still lamenting the loss of her dream of having a quality time out with her son, It's okay, your son loves you.

Don't give up hope, mom holding back your tears after another treatment report that makes you feel like your kid isn't improving!

Not by yourself! Remember that you're not alone when you're trying to keep going or when it seems bleak. I want you to keep in mind that you're doing a fantastic job when you feel like no one sees you until your kid is crying or when you're unsure of how you're going to manage it any longer. You are trying your best to raise your kid, and I know you adore them. Remember that I

understand what you're going through and
that there are many others who do as well.